TEST 1

聽力：是非題

作答說明：每題你將會聽到 1 個短句。請仔細聽，聽到的句子和圖片是不是相同呢？如果相同，請在答案卡上塗黑 Y；如果不同，請塗黑 N。

錄音內容：They are in an electronic store.

正確答案：Y

1.

Taipei

2. Ⓨ Ⓝ

3. Ⓨ Ⓝ

4.

5. Ⓨ Ⓝ

6. Ⓨ Ⓝ

7. Ⓨ Ⓝ

8.  Ⓨ Ⓝ

9. Ⓨ Ⓝ

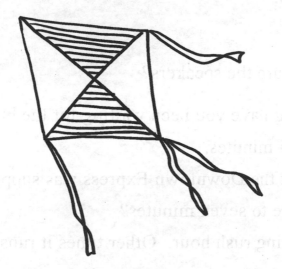

10.

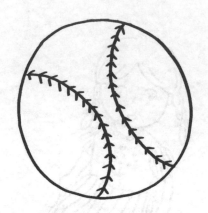

聽力：選擇題

<u>作答說明</u>：每題你將會聽到 1 段對話，每段對話開始前，你會先聽到和看到一個問題。請仔細聽問題和對話，並選一個最適合的答案，在答案卡上塗黑作答。

Where are the speakers?
A. At school.
B. At a bus stop.
C. At a gym.

錄音內容：Where are the speakers?

Boy ： How long have you been waiting for the bus?

Girl ： About 15 minutes.

Boy ： I thought the Downtown Express was supposed to run every five to seven minutes?

Girl ： Only during rush hour. Other times it runs every 20 minutes.

正確答案：B

11. Why did David's father stay at home?

    A. He missed the train.

    B. He is not feeling well.

    C. No, he's not home.

12. Why do the speakers like their teacher?

    A. She is patient and kind.

    B. They don't like her.

    C. Yes, they like her.

13. How often does the woman use her computer?

    A. Seldom.

    B. Every day.

    C. Often.

14. Where are the speakers?

    A. In a cafeteria.

    B. In a theater.

    C. In a library.

15. What does the girl want to do?

    A. Go to sleep.

    B. Watch a movie.

    C. Finish her homework.

16. What will the man do this weekend?

    A. Take an exam.

    B. Go to the beach.

    C. Study for an exam.

17. What is the woman doing?

    A. Looking for a boyfriend.

    B. Going overseas.

    C. Writing a letter.

18. Where are they?

    A. In a restaurant.

    B. In the country.

    C. In the kitchen.

19. Where is the man going?

    A. To his office.

    B. To the hospital and the supermarket.

    C. To the cleaners and the post office.

20. Why doesn't the man eat the pizza?

    A. He has to go to work.

    B. He is on a diet.

    C. He doesn't like pizza.

TEST 2

聽力：是非題

作答說明：每題你將會聽到 1 個短句。請仔細聽，聽到的句子和圖片是不是相同呢？如果相同，請在答案卡上塗黑 Y；如果不同，請塗黑 N。

錄音內容：They are in an electronic store.

正確答案：Y

1. (Y)　(N)

2.

3.

4.

5. Y   N

6.

7.

8.

9. (Y) (N)

10. Ⓨ Ⓝ

聽力：選擇題

作答說明：每題你將會聽到 1 段對話，每段對話開始前，你會先聽到和看到一個問題。請仔細聽問題和對話，<u>並選一個最適合的答案</u>，在答案卡上塗黑作答。

Where are the speakers?
A. At school.
B. At a bus stop.
C. At a gym.

錄音內容：Where are the speakers?

Boy ：How long have you been waiting for the bus?

Girl ：About 15 minutes.

Boy ：I thought the Downtown Express was supposed to run every five to seven minutes?

Girl ：Only during rush hour. Other times it runs every 20 minutes.

正確答案：B

11. What are they talking about?

    A. The man's watch.

    B. The woman's mother.

    C. The department store.

12. Did Cindy have a good day?

    A. Yes, she feels great.

    B. It was Monday.

    C. No. She had a bad day.

13. Where are they?

    A. In a library.

    B. In a train station.

    C. In a restaurant.

14. Did the girl win a race?

    A. No, she didn't.

    B. Yes. She won the 100-meter race.

    C. She didn't run in the race.

15. Will the man have an exam tomorrow?

    A. No. He doesn't have any questions.

    B. No, he doesn't want to have an exam.

    C. Yes, he will have an exam.

16. What did the woman buy at the department store?

    A. A new dress.

    B. Everything she wanted.

    C. Nothing.

17. Can the man speak French?

    A. He lives in France.

    B. Yes, he can speak some French.

    C. No. He has never been to France.

18. What do we know about George?

    A. He is in the hospital.

    B. He was fighting at school.

    C. He was the best student in class.

19. What is Alien Zombies?

    A. A song.

    B. A painting.

    C. A movie.

20. What did the man do?

    A. He found a kitten.

    B. He bought a dog.

    C. He made a new friend.

TEST 3

聽力：是非題

作答說明：每題你將會聽到 1 個短句。請仔細聽，聽到的句子和圖片是不
是相同呢？如果相同，請在答案卡上塗黑 Y；如果不同，請塗黑 N。

錄音內容：They are in an electronic store.

正確答案：Y

1.

2. (Y) (N)

Peter

3. (Y) (N)

4.

Mr. Martin

5.

6.

7.

8.

KNSH NEWS

9. Y N

10.

聽力：選擇題

作答說明：每題你將會聽到 1 段對話，每段對話開始前，你會先聽到和看到一個問題。請仔細聽問題和對話，並選一個最適合的答案，在答案卡上塗黑作答。

Where are the speakers?
A. At school.
B. At a bus stop.
C. At a gym.

錄音內容：Where are the speakers?

Boy：How long have you been waiting for the bus?

Girl：About 15 minutes.

Boy：I thought the Downtown Express was supposed to run every five to seven minutes?

Girl：Only during rush hour. Other times it runs every 20 minutes.

正確答案：B

11. Who is the woman?

    A. The man's mail carrier.

    B. The man's wife.

    C. The man's neighbor.

12. What did the woman buy?

    A. A red shirt.

    B. 200 shirts.

    C. Nothing.

13. Where are they?

    A. In a classroom.

    B. In an ice cream shop.

    C. In the woman's home.

14. How does Joe look?

    A. Tall and handsome.

    B. Not special at all.

    C. Like a girl.

15. When should you eat cherries?

    A. Winter.

    B. Summer.

    C. Right now.

16. What does the man do?

    A. Lend money to the woman.

    B. Leave a message.

    C. Go home.

17. How often does the man smoke?

    A. Every day.

    B. Never.

    C. Sometimes.

18. Why did the woman leave the party?

    A. She was sick.

    B. She wasn't invited.

    C. She wasn't having fun.

19. What did the woman do yesterday?

    A. She started a new job.

    B. She moved to a different city.

    C. She stopped working.

20. What is true about both speakers?

    A. They are at the Tonghua Night Market.

    B. Both are new in town.

    C. Both travel by boat.

TEST 4

聽力：是非題

作答說明：每題你將會聽到 1 個短句。請仔細聽，聽到的句子和圖片是不是相同呢？如果相同，請在答案卡上塗黑 Y；如果不同，請塗黑 N。

錄音內容：They are in an electronic store.

正確答案：Y

1. Ⓨ Ⓝ

2.

3.

4. (Y) (N)

5. (Y) (N)

6.

7.

8.

9. (Y) (N)

10. Ⓨ Ⓝ

聽力：選擇題

作答說明：每題你將會聽到 1 段對話，每段對話開始前，你會先聽到和看到一個問題。請仔細聽問題和對話，並選一個最適合的答案，在答案卡上塗黑作答。

Where are the speakers?
A. At school.
B. At a bus stop.
C. At a gym.

錄音內容：Where are the speakers?

Boy ：How long have you been waiting for the bus?

Girl ：About 15 minutes.

Boy ：I thought the Downtown Express was supposed to run every five to seven minutes?

Girl ：Only during rush hour. Other times it runs every 20 minutes.

正確答案：B

11. What should the man do?

    A. Go on vacation.

    B. Get a haircut.

    C. Wash his hair.

12. When will the woman and man have a meeting?

    A. This afternoon.

    B. They won't have a meeting.

    C. Tomorrow morning.

13. What did the boy do yesterday?

    A. He gave the woman some money.

    B. He broke the woman's window.

    C. He won a baseball game.

14. What is the woman holding?

    A. A ladder.

    B. Her arms.

    C. A clock.

15. What are the speakers doing?

    A. Riding a bus.

    B. Flying a plane.

    C. Driving a car.

16. What was Robert's grade on the test?

    A. He got an A-plus.

    B. He didn't take the test.

    C. He got an F.

17. Do the speakers know each other?

    A. No. They are meeting for the first time.

    B. Yes. They are classmates.

    C. No. They are cousins.

18. What does the man say about Mr. Simon?

    A. He will order for him.

    B. He's always late.

    C. He always answers his phone.

19. What does the woman want?

    A. She wants to talk with the man now.

    B. She wants to be quiet.

    C. She wants to go to the doctor.

20. Where does the man want to go?

    A. To a job interview.

    B. To the airport.

    C. To his school.

TEST 5

聽力：是非題

作答說明：每題你將會聽到 1 個短句。請仔細聽，聽到的句子和圖片是不是相同呢？如果相同，請在答案卡上塗黑 Y；如果不同，請塗黑 N。

錄音內容：They are in an electronic store.

正確答案：Y

1. (Y) (N)

7月
19
星期六

2. （Y）　（N）

3. （Y）　（N）

4.

5. **Y** **N**

6. Ⓨ Ⓝ

7. Ⓨ Ⓝ

8. 

9. **Y** **N**

10. Ⓨ Ⓝ

聽力：選擇題

作答說明：每題你將會聽到 1 段對話，每段對話開始前，你會先聽到和看到一個問題。請仔細聽問題和對話，並選一個最適合的答案，在答案卡上塗黑作答。

Where are the speakers?
A. At school.
B. At a bus stop.
C. At a gym.

錄音內容：Where are the speakers?

Boy ：How long have you been waiting for the bus?

Girl ：About 15 minutes.

Boy ：I thought the Downtown Express was supposed to run every five to seven minutes?

Girl ：Only during rush hour. Other times it runs every 20 minutes.

正確答案：B

11. What is the problem?

    A. The woman's dog is too noisy.

    B. The man lost his dog.

    C. The woman does not have a dog.

12. What is Lisa doing?

    A. Sleeping.

    B. Using her computer.

    C. Listening to music.

13. Who is the man?

    A. An artist.

    B. A shopkeeper.

    C. A farmer.

14. How old is the girl?

    A. She is 20 years old.

    B. She is 12 years old.

    C. She is 11 years old.

15. Who is the man?

    A. A bus driver.

    B. A teacher.

    C. A police officer.

16. What do we know about the man?

    A. He was on vacation.

    B. He is a doctor.

    C. His was sick.

17. Why is the woman worried?

    A. Her son has poor grades.

    B. She doesn't have a boyfriend.

    C. Her son has a girlfriend.

18. What are the speakers talking about?

    A. How much money they spend.

    B. Shopping on the Internet.

    C. Which department store to go to.

19. What will the man give Danny?

    A. A water gun.

    B. Money.

    C. A birthday cake.

20. What does the man want to do?

    A. Buy a shirt.

    B. Pay three hundred dollars.

    C. Find a different shirt.

TEST 6

聽力：是非題

作答說明：每題你將會聽到 1 個短句。請仔細聽，聽到的句子和圖片是不是相同呢？如果相同，請在答案卡上塗黑 Y；如果不同，請塗黑 N。

錄音內容：They are in an electronic store.

正確答案：Y

1.

2.

3.

4.

5. Y N

6.

7. **Y** **N**

8.  Y N

9. Y N

10. (Y) (N)

聽力：選擇題

作答說明：每題你將會聽到 1 段對話，每段對話開始前，你會先聽到和看到一個問題。請仔細聽問題和對話，並選一個最適合的答案，在答案卡上塗黑作答。

Where are the speakers?
A. At school.
B. At a bus stop.
C. At a gym.

錄音內容：Where are the speakers?

Boy ：How long have you been waiting for the bus?

Girl ：About 15 minutes.

Boy ：I thought the Downtown Express was supposed to run every five to seven minutes?

Girl ：Only during rush hour. Other times it runs every 20 minutes.

正確答案：B

11. Who is the girl?

   A. An old friend.

   B. A new student.

   C. A popular teacher.

12. Why is Scott's mother angry?

   A. Scott is eating a sandwich.

   B. Scott didn't take off his shoes.

   C. Scott came home late.

13. When will the woman come back?

   A. She will stay.

   B. This afternoon.

   C. Tomorrow morning.

14. Why does Julie feel sad?

   A. She hurt herself.

   B. She is in the hospital.

   C. Her cat died.

15. What is the man doing?

   A. Studying.

   B. Listening to music.

   C. Watching TV.

16. Does the man like Larry Smith?

    A. He thinks Larry is nice.

    B. No, he doesn't.

    C. He likes Larry a lot.

17. What is the girl worried about?

    A. A strange man at the door.

    B. A loud noise in the bathroom.

    C. A dog in the front yard.

18. What did the woman do in Hualien?

    A. She went shopping.

    B. She went hiking and swimming.

    C. She went fishing.

19. How much does the scarf cost?

    A. Four hundred dollars.

    B. It's not expensive.

    C. $950.

20. What are the speakers talking about?

    A. Their school.

    B. Their vacation.

    C. Their son, Tommy.

TEST 7

聽力：是非題

作答說明：每題你將會聽到 1 個短句。請仔細聽，聽到的句子和圖片是不是相同呢？如果相同，請在答案卡上塗黑 Y；如果不同，請塗黑 N。

錄音內容：They are in an electronic store.

正確答案：Y

1.

2. (Y) (N)

3. (Y) (N)

4. (Y) (N)

5. (Y) (N)

6. Ⓨ Ⓝ

7. Ⓨ Ⓝ

8.  Ⓨ Ⓝ

9. Ⓨ Ⓝ

10. Ⓨ Ⓝ

聽力：選擇題

作答說明：每題你將會聽到 1 段對話，每段對話開始前，你會先聽到和看到一個問題。請仔細聽問題和對話，並選一個最適合的答案，在答案卡上塗黑作答。

Where are the speakers?
A. At school.
B. At a bus stop.
C. At a gym.

錄音內容：Where are the speakers?

Boy：How long have you been waiting for the bus?

Girl：About 15 minutes.

Boy：I thought the Downtown Express was supposed to run every five to seven minutes?

Girl：Only during rush hour. Other times it runs every 20 minutes.

正確答案：B

11. What is the man doing?

    A. Cooking dinner.

    B. Eating a piece of pie.

    C. Cleaning up the kitchen.

12. Why are the speakers worried?

    A. They smelled smoke.

    B. They heard a loud noise.

    C. They saw a stranger at the door.

13. Who is Champ?

    A. A friend.

    B. A family member.

    C. A pet.

14. Why was the man late?

    A. The traffic was bad.

    B. He forgot the date.

    C. His car did not start.

15. What will the speakers do this weekend?

    A. Go to a movie festival.

    B. Go shopping.

    C. Visit another country.

16. How does Amy feel about her summer vacation?

    A.　It was too long.

    B.　It was too hot.

    C.　It was too short.

17. Where does the woman want to go?

    A.　To the museum.

    B.　To the zoo.

    C.　To the bank.

18. Does the man like the woman's dress?

    A.　No, he doesn't.

    B.　Yes, he does.

    C.　It's impossible to say.

19. What time does George need to leave the house?

    A.　Midnight.

    B.　4:00 a.m.

    C.　3:00 p.m.

20. Who left the back door open?

    A.　The man.

    B.　The woman.

    C.　The cat.

TEST 8

作答說明：每題你將會聽到 1 個短句。請仔細聽，聽到的句子和圖片是不是相同呢？如果相同，請在答案卡上塗黑 Y；如果不同，請塗黑 N。

錄音內容：They are in an electronic store.

正確答案：Y

1. Ⓨ Ⓝ

2. Ⓨ Ⓝ

3. Ⓨ Ⓝ

4.

5.

日	一	二	三	四	五	六
			1	2	3	4
5	6	7	8	9	10	11
12	13	14	15	16	17	18
19	20	21	22	23	24	25
26	27	28	29	30	31	

6.

7. Y N

8.

9. Y N

10.

聽力：選擇題

作答說明：每題你將會聽到 1 段對話，每段對話開始前，你會先聽到和看到一個問題。請仔細聽問題和對話，並選一個最適合的答案，在答案卡上塗黑作答。

Where are the speakers?
A. At school.
B. At a bus stop.
C. At a gym.

錄音內容：Where are the speakers?

Boy ：How long have you been waiting for the bus?

Girl ：About 15 minutes.

Boy ：I thought the Downtown Express was supposed to run every five to seven minutes?

Girl ：Only during rush hour. Other times it runs every 20 minutes.

正確答案：B

11. When will they go swimming?

   A. Tomorrow morning.

   B. Tomorrow afternoon.

   C. Tomorrow evening.

12. Has the girl finished her homework?

   A. No, she hasn't.

   B. Yes, she has.

   C. I don't know.

13. How much does the ferry boat cost on Wednesday?

   A. 50 dollars each way.

   B. 120 dollars.

   C. 60 dollars each way.

14. How often does the woman eat at the restaurant?

   A. Often.

   B. Sometimes.

   C. Seldom.

15. Where are they?

   A. In a cafeteria.

   B. In a library.

   C. In a classroom.

16. Will there be a game today?

    A. Yes, there will.

    B. No, there won't.

    C. Sometimes there is.

17. Does the woman know Jack Forrest?

    A. Yes, because she is Jack's sister.

    B. Yes, she knows him very well.

    C. No, but she knows Jack's sister.

18. What did the woman borrow?

    A. A computer.

    B. A calculator.

    C. A pencil.

19. What color shirt does the man want?

    A. Black.

    B. White.

    C. Blue.

20. Will the man go hiking tomorrow?

    A. Yes, if it is not raining.

    B. No, definitely not.

    C. No, because he does not like hiking.

TEST 9

錄音內容：They are in an electronic store.

正確答案：Y

1.

2. Ⓨ Ⓝ

3. Ⓨ Ⓝ

4. Y N

5. Y N

6.

7.

8.

9.

10. Ⓨ Ⓝ

聽力：選擇題

作答說明：每題你將會聽到 1 段對話，每段對話開始前，你會先聽到和看到一個問題。請仔細聽問題和對話，並選一個最適合的答案，在答案卡上塗黑作答。

Where are the speakers?
A. At school.
B. At a bus stop.
C. At a gym.

錄音內容： Where are the speakers?

Boy：How long have you been waiting for the bus?

Girl：About 15 minutes.

Boy：I thought the Downtown Express was supposed to run every five to seven minutes?

Girl：Only during rush hour. Other times it runs every 20 minutes.

正確答案： B

11. What are they doing?

   A. Cleaning.

   B. Planning a party.

   C. Having a party.

12. What is Tom doing?

   A. Sleeping.

   B. Eating.

   C. Reading.

13. What is the girl doing?

   A. Planning a trip.

   B. Studying for a test.

   C. Going abroad.

14. What does the woman like to read about?

   A. Comics.

   B. Novels.

   C. History and science.

15. What are they talking about?

   A. Their teacher.

   B. Their homework.

   C. A Christmas party.

16. Who is the woman?

    A. The boss.

    B. A customer.

    C. The man's daughter.

17. Did the man give the woman her change?

    A. No, the man forgot to give the woman her change.

    B. No. The woman does not need any change.

    C. Yes, the man gave her the change.

18. What is expensive in New York?

    A. Taxis.

    B. Hotels.

    C. Food.

19. Will the woman study tonight?

    A. Yes, she will.

    B. No, she won't.

    C. Maybe, she did.

20. Where did the conversation take place?

    A. On the street.

    B. In a library.

    C. On an airplane.

TEST 10

聽力：是非題

錄音內容：They are in an electronic store.

正確答案：Y

1. （Y）（N）

2. Y N

3. Y N

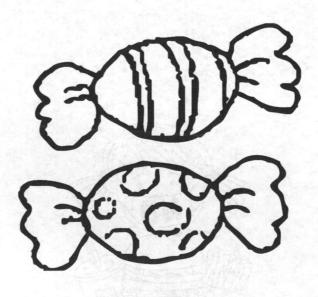

4.

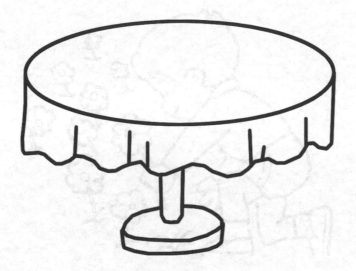

5. **Y** **N**

6.

7.

8. (Y) (N)

9. (Y) (N)

10. Ⓨ Ⓝ

聽力：選擇題

作答說明：每題你將會聽到 1 段對話，每段對話開始前，你會先聽到和看到一個問題。請仔細聽問題和對話，並選一個最適合的答案，在答案卡上塗黑作答。

Where are the speakers?
A. At school.
B. At a bus stop.
C. At a gym.

錄音內容：Where are the speakers?

Boy ：How long have you been waiting for the bus?

Girl ：About 15 minutes.

Boy ：I thought the Downtown Express was supposed to run every five to seven minutes?

Girl ：Only during rush hour. Other times it runs every 20 minutes.

正確答案：B

11. Why is the woman in a hurry?

    A. She's late for work.

    B. She's late for school.

    C. She's late for a party.

12. What day is it?

    A. Friday.

    B. Saturday.

    C. Sunday.

13. When will the woman arrive at the bus station?

    A. Before sunset.

    B. After midnight.

    C. Noon.

14. What does the man think the woman should wear?

    A. The short dress.

    B. The long skirt.

    C. Jeans.

15. Is Peter tall?

    A. No, he isn't.

    B. Sometimes, he will.

    C. Yes, he is.

16. What did the girl do?

    A. She turned on the radio.

    B. She went to bed.

    C. She finished her homework.

17. Who has been to Japan?

    A. The man.

    B. The woman.

    C. Both the man and the woman.

18. Where are they?

    A. On a bus.

    B. At the train station.

    C. At home.

19. What happened last night?

    A. The man took his daughter to the hospital.

    B. The woman's son got very ill.

    C. The man called the woman.

20. Will the woman buy milk at the market?

    A. No. She will buy coffee.

    B. She will not go to the market.

    C. Yes, she will.

TEST 11

聽力：是非題

作答說明：每題你將會聽到 1 個短句。請仔細聽，聽到的句子和圖片是不
是相同呢？如果相同，請在答案卡上塗黑 Y；如果不同，請塗黑 N。

錄音內容：They are in an electronic store.

正確答案：Y

1.

2.

3.

4.  Y N

5. Y N

6. (Y) (N)

7. (Y) (N)

Name	Age	Food	Color	Sport
Donny	8	Juice	Pink	Baseball
Pam	10	Ice cream	Green	Basketball
Sandy	12	Chicken	Purple	Dodge ball
Ben	12	Pizza	Orange	Swim

8.  Y N

9.  Y N

10. Ⓨ Ⓝ

聽力：選擇題

作答說明：每題你將會聽到 1 段對話，每段對話開始前，你會先聽到和看到一個問題。請仔細聽問題和對話，並選一個最適合的答案，在答案卡上塗黑作答。

Where are the speakers?
A. At school.
B. At a bus stop.
C. At a gym.

錄音內容： Where are the speakers?

Boy：How long have you been waiting for the bus?

Girl：About 15 minutes.

Boy：I thought the Downtown Express was supposed to run every five to seven minutes?

Girl：Only during rush hour. Other times it runs every 20 minutes.

正確答案：B

11. What will cost 14,000 dollars?

    A. Calling the woman's husband.

    B. The woman's vacation.

    C. Fixing the woman's car.

12. What is Bob's problem?

    A. He is bored.

    B. He is too busy.

    C. His stomach hurts.

13. Where is the woman?

    A. At a restaurant.

    B. Out of town.

    C. At the office.

14. Will Betty ask Mike to do something?

    A. No, she won't.

    B. Yes, she will.

    C. Yes, she was.

15. Why didn't the woman eat the cookies?

    A. She is on a diet.

    B. She has a toothache.

    C. She will go to the dentist later in the day.

16. What is the man?

  A. A writer.

  B. A teacher.

  C. A college student.

17. What does the man want?

  A. He wants to buy a smartphone.

  B. He wants to sell his watch.

  C. He wants to sign a contract.

18. Where are they?

  A. In a bank.

  B. In a library.

  C. In a restaurant.

19. What is the woman looking for?

  A. Her friend.

  B. The hospital.

  C. A train station.

20. What time is it now?

  A. Eight o'clock.

  B. Ten o'clock.

  C. Eleven o'clock.

TEST 12

聽力：是非題

作答說明：每題你將會聽到 1 個短句。請仔細聽，聽到的句子和圖片是不是相同呢？如果相同，請在答案卡上塗黑 Y；如果不同，請塗黑 N。

錄音內容：They are in an electronic store.

正確答案：Y

1. Ⓨ Ⓝ

2.

3. (Y) (N)

4.

5.

6.

7.

8. (Y) (N)

9. (Y) (N)

10. (Y) (N)

聽力：選擇題

作答說明：每題你將會聽到 1 段對話，每段對話開始前，你會先聽到和看到一個問題。請仔細聽問題和對話，並選一個最適合的答案，在答案卡上塗黑作答。

Where are the speakers?
A. At school.
B. At a bus stop.
C. At a gym.

錄音內容：Where are the speakers?

Boy : How long have you been waiting for the bus?

Girl : About 15 minutes.

Boy : I thought the Downtown Express was supposed to run every five to seven minutes?

Girl : Only during rush hour. Other times it runs every 20 minutes.

正確答案：B

11. What did the boy do with his dishes?

    A. He used a bowl.

    B. He put them in the sink.

    C. He didn't have any dishes.

12. What time is it now?

    A. 4:00.

    B. 4:40.

    C. 5:00.

13. How much does delivery cost?

    A. Nothing.

    B. 500 dollars.

    C. There is no delivery service.

14. What does the man want?

    A. A small sweater in blue.

    B. A large jacket in red.

    C. A green shirt or a blue shirt.

15. Is Mr. Collins in the office?

    A. Yes, he's at his desk.

    B. No, he's not in the office.

    C. No, but he left a message.

16. What happened to the woman?

    A. She fell off her bike.

    B. She fell off a ladder.

    C. She fell down the stairs.

17. Is the man afraid of heights?

    A. Yes, he is.

    B. No, he isn't.

    C. Sometimes, he does.

18. What time does the party start?

    A. Seven o'clock.

    B. Eight o'clock.

    C. When the movie ends.

19. What does the man tell the woman to do?

    A. Unplug the computer.

    B. Restart the computer.

    C. Call a repairman.

20. What is the woman's score on the entrance exam?

    A. She did well.

    B. She did poorly.

    C. She doesn't know her score yet.